Nicholas
from ♡ S0-CEY-858
Grandpa Shaffer Easter 1986

DISNEY'S
ELEGANT
BOOK OF
MANNERS

DISNEY'S ELEGANT BOOK OF MANNERS

Written by
VINCENT JEFFERDS

A Little Simon Book
Published by Simon & Schuster, Inc.

Copyright © 1985 by Walt Disney Productions
All rights reserved including the right of reproduction in whole or in part in any form.
Published by LITTLE SIMON, a Division of Simon & Schuster.
Simon & Schuster Building, 1230 Avenue of the Americas, New York, New York 10020
LITTLE SIMON and colophon are trademarks of Simon & Schuster. Printed in the United States of America.
10 9 8 7 6 5 4 3 2 1
ISBN: 0-671-60507-0

In the beginning...

The manners of early man
    Were really not much better than
Those of beasts who ruled by might
    And had no thought of wrong or right.

Man was nothing to rave about,
Short on manners, long on clout.

If you didn't share his point of view,
He was apt to raise a lump on you.

He stayed busy hunting game,
And he moved a lot, chasing same.

Man was a nomadic race,
Moving on from place to place.
In the woods and on the plain,
He searched for berries, nuts, and game.

Man improved the human race
When he settled in one place.
He raised livestock in his stables,
And planted food and ate at tables.
This quickly led him to discover
Rules for living with each other.

Manners weren't simply invented
    So young people could be tormented
By grown-up folks who never miss
    A chance to say, "Do that and this."

Manners are the social mold
    That fits the same for young or old.
Manners are man's best creation
    For showing each other consideration.

It's nicer to ask than to demand,
That's something we all understand.

If Donald shouts, "I want a bun,"
I probably wouldn't give him one.

But if Mickey says, "Please pass the tea,"
I'd give him a pot as tall as he.

Here's a bit of sound advice:
When some good friend does something nice,
A "Thank you" makes it understood
That what he's done makes you feel good.
For both of you it's much more fun
If you say thanks for what he's done.
(And it will be much sooner when
He does something nice again.)

"You're welcome" is the right response,
And if you're smart, it's done at once.

If you spill your cone on someone's dress,
And the ice cream makes an awful mess,
Saying "I'm sorry" will not clean it,
But it tells her that you didn't mean it.

You can be angry at a crook
   If he tries to steal your book.

Once in a while is not out of line,
   But if you lose your temper all the time,
And friends must hear you scream and shout,
   I'm afraid you'll wear their patience out.

Though Tommy Jones had surely grown some,
In a crowd he still felt lonesome.
He didn't know that looking grim
Kept folks from speaking up to him.

To keep from staying on the sidelines,
Follow certain simple guidelines.

The thing you must remember is,
A smile and a word or two
Is what the other person
Would like to get from you.

If you sneeze and you cough and your nose
    starts to swell,
    Please stay at home until you get well.
With all your friends, you'll stay on good terms
    If you don't go among them spreading your germs.

When you're sick at home, you must remember,
    It means more work for some family member.
So don't be cranky—cooperate.
    It's something Mom will appreciate.

Bravely take the goo and pills,
    To speed the exit of your ills.
Don't push your mother to the limit,
    By yelling for service every minute.

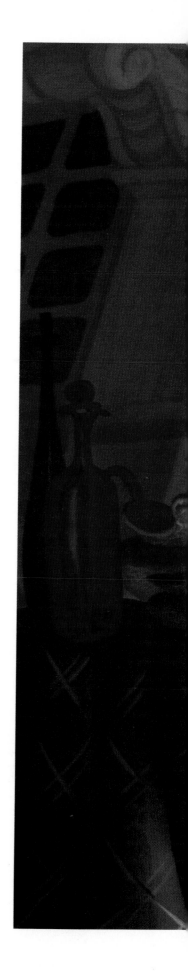

People come in every shape and size,
    They can't all be pleasing to your eyes.

If you meet someone odd someday,
    Don't comment on his looks.
Just act in a normal, natural way—
    You've seen worse in comic books.

Keeping the whole earth clean starts with
  you.
When you're older there'll be more that you
  can do
To help find some good solutions
  To the terrible problem of pollution.

The things that you own are entrusted to you.
Don't neglect or abuse them, whatever you do.

Leave your bike out in the rain,
And it will never be the same.

Your neighbor's lawn is clean and fresh.
You wouldn't want to soil it.
So please be sure that dog of yours
Doesn't use it as a toilet.

Spit is called expectorate.
   Use a tissue, not the street.
That is, if you expect to rate
   With people who are clean and neat.

You can pick a shoe
  That's right for you.
You can pick a friend,
  And you won't offend.
You can pick a peach,
  If it's in your reach.

But whether we say it in poem or prose,
Never, oh never, pick your nose.

The good fairy warned Pinocchio
    That if he lied his nose would grow.
It did, so then he understood
    That it was better to be good.
And when he was good, to his great joy,
    She made of him a real, live boy.

Even if your nose won't grow,
    Like it did with Pinocchio,
It's important that you try
    Not to tell your friends a lie.

Don't interrupt when someone's talking,
That's something you should learn.
They'll finish talking soon enough,
And then you'll get your turn.

Nasty remarks will never work.
Be kind when you speak of another.

You may tell someone Tom's a jerk,
And find you're talking to his brother.

Don't just drop in on someone.
    Please call him in advance.
It may be inconvenient,
    Or he may be out, by chance.

Why knock before entering someone's room?
The answer you have guessed:
She may not wish to be disturbed
Because she's getting dressed.

If you're playing music in your room,
  I suggest you keep it down.
It doesn't have to roar and boom
  So loud that it's heard downtown.

If you play too loud, I fear
You could also damage your inner ear.

When you are eating with a group,
Do not blow upon your soup.

Speaking as a general rule,
   Soups are like hot-tempered fools.
You need only wait for them to cool.

Before a bus trip, please arrange
	To get there with the proper change.
If you don't, it's no disaster,
	But when you do, the line moves faster.

You can make more room up front, my dear,
	By moving quickly to the rear.

On a bus, there's nothing worse than
	Taking a seat from an older person.

Always enter single file,
  So that you do not block the aisle.
If you're flying, please refrain
  From running up and down the plane.

With a phone, what you need to know,
Is pick it up and say "Hello."
If it's for Dad from Uncle Jim,
Say "Please hold on. I'll go get him."

Of course that's not the thing to say,
If for the moment Dad's away,
In which case you say, "Uncle Jim,
May I take a message for him?"

It's not difficult to share
When you have a lot to spare.

But if you share when there is less,
Then you are truly generous.

Your fame will not become undone
If you don't boast when you have won.

Bad losers don't get invited out to dinner,
  So smile, and congratulate the winner.
It was said by a man of lasting fame,
  "It's not who wins, but how you play the game."
But don't be fooled, it's not the same:

Even if the odds seem slim,
Play with the thought that you can win.

Join in games that please the rest,
Don't always choose what you like best.

It is always fun to win a lot,
    But there's no reason that you've got
To always play with someone younger,
    Or always play with someone dumber.

If you're at the beach
   And you want to run races,
Don't jump over folks
   And kick sand in their faces.

A crowded sidewalk's not the place
For a roller-skating race.

If you have a bike, you deserve a medal
If you are careful where you pedal.

Strangers are people not known to you,
    And whatever they tell you may be untrue.
So don't do what they ask you to
    Even if they are older than you.

If a stranger offers food or candy,
    Get away as fast as can be.
It might be a dirty trick,
    And eating it could make you sick.

Strangers might want to hurt you, so
    Don't be afraid to tell them no.

Remember, you must never go
    In a car with someone you don't know.

If someone offers you a ride,
    Keep walking. Never get inside.

If you're home alone,
  Don't open the door,
Unless it's someone
  You've met before.

Don't leave your room in disarray.
Keep it neat; put things away.
A little care from you, and then
It won't look like an old pigpen.

Another thing to learn real soon
Is to do your share in the bathroom.

The tube expects to be capped, so don't confuse it,

And clean the bathtub after you use it.

Snow White treated the dwarfs with friendliness,
  But she always insisted on cleanliness.
So, as long as she was there,
  They washed their faces and combed their hair.
And she gave extra cake to the daily winner
  Who washed the best before eating dinner.

There was an old woman who lived in a shoe,
　　She had so many children, she didn't know what to do.
So she washed them, and fed them, and tucked them in bed;
　　She had no time for stories. What she did, instead,
Was to teach them good manners and plenty of jokes,
　　And they all grew up into very nice folks.

Jack Sprat could eat no fat,
   His wife could eat no lean.
And that is why between the two,
   They licked the platter clean.

Jack Sprat is lean and spry,
   His health is very sound.
Mrs. Sprat has gotten fat,
   She can hardly get around.

Something we learn from this is that
   It's not too smart to get too fat.
And then there is that other matter,
   One should never lick a plate or platter.

Hey Diddle, Diddle, the plate's in the middle,
To the right is the knife and the spoon.
The little fork laughed to see such fun,
When the dish ran away with the spoon.

We don't care if they're not back yet.
They're both odd pieces from a kitchen set.

Now's a good time to tell you a fable,
    How knife, fork, and spoon first came to the table.
A spear maker, who was a clever old soul,
    Was tired of grabbing his food from a bowl.

And so he stayed up all one night,
    And designed some cutlery. He did it right—
He designed a knife and fork and spoon,
    Then fell asleep and slept till noon.

When he fell asleep, he dreamed:
   The knife stood up and talked, it seemed,
And all of them had just begun
   To argue who was number one.

"I," said the knife, "am number one.
    Without my blade no cut is done."
"Humph," said the fork, "go ask your wife
    To eat her peas on the blade of a knife.
And I'll give you another tip—
    A knife might even cut her lip."

"Well," said the spoon, "you're great with pork,
    But try to eat your soup with a fork!"

And then when they had thought a while,
   They agreed they each had a special style,
And what they really had to face,
   Was where each had its proper place.

When he awoke, his gaze then met
   A table that was neatly set.
"I think it looks just right to me;
   That's the way it ought to be."

Of course, the old man was, like most,
   An average, right-handed host.
So for left-handed folks, I fear,
   It's been an awkward setting many years.

Most people have more skill and heft
  In their right hand than in their left.
So knife and spoon are to the right,
  Opposite the right hand, in plain sight.

bread and butter plate
  and spreader

dinner plate

teacup and saucer

salad

napkin

din

water goblet

teaspoon

knife

ork

To the left the fork is set,
    To hold the food while being cut.
Then to eat, the rules demand
    You shift the fork to your right hand.

The napkin is to clean yourself,
  As you will soon perceive.
You can use it to wipe your face and mouth,
  Instead of using your sleeve.

When you handle food, some of it lingers,
  But you must never lick it from your fingers.
We say it now, as we said before,
  "That's what the napkin's invented for."

I'm afraid you will look like a dunce,
    If you cut all your meat up at once.
Cut one piece and eat it, then
    Cut yourself a piece again.

Don't push food on your fork with your fingers. Instead
Use a piece of a roll or a cracker or bread.

Pets are one of life's great joys,
　　But just remember they're not toys.
We must ask you, without fail,
　　Never pull an animal's tail.
You wouldn't think that it was fun
　　If, for a moment, you had one.

Pets give you fun, it's only fair
  That you give them the proper care.
Don't forget, they need to be
  Cleaned and fed regularly.

Eat your soup like tiny Roo.
When you spoon a little sip,
Make the motion away from you.
Thus you avoid the spill and drip.

Remove your spoon after you mix,
Or you might be in Donald's fix.

Whether you have tea with Alice,
  In your home or in a palace.
Or with a hare or with a hatter,
  How you pour will always matter.
Just be sure to aim the spout,
  Before a drop of tea comes out.
Another caution that we bid
  Is to keep a finger on the lid.

At your age you might ask why
   You ever would give snails a try.
But to say "never" is always hasty.
   Someday you'll find they are quite tasty.

In any case the tools are fun,
   And can be learned by anyone.
A pair of forceps holds the shell,
   And a tiny fork will dig quite well.
Then the snail gives up its lease,
   And comes out neatly in one piece.

It is neat, and
   It is great
If you take what you need
   And don't pile your plate.

Don't sit too far away from the table.
Sit up close, like John and Mabel,
Or you'll find when you reach for bread,
It may land on the floor instead.

Don't slouch in your seat when you eat.
If you lean back and tilt the chair,
You'll be the first one to eat
With your feet tilted up in the air.

See how fast he cleans his plate—
He could win a prize for speed.
He should eat his meal at a slower rate,
And enjoy it more, indeed.

Don't toy with food upon your plate,
Or you will find that you are late.
When all the other folks are through,
They don't want to wait for you.

If the only way that you feel stable,
Is to eat with elbows on the table,

It may be you need a rest,
And leaving the table would be best.

Most folks consider that someone is rude
   If he tries to talk with a mouthful of food.
Your mouth is designed to talk and to eat,
   But to do both at once is a difficult feat.
The only exception (I say this in fun)
   Is a guest with two heads instead of one.

Avoid, as much as you are able,
 Unpleasant subjects at the table,
Like how you took Dad's pipe and washed it,
 Or stepped on a katydid and squashed it.

These are not things worth repeating
 While dinner guests of yours are eating.

A pig is cute, a pig is fun,
But I wouldn't want to look like one.
It's an impression hard to erase
If when you eat, you stuff your face.

Dogs and cats may gulp their meal
  As fast as they are able.
But how do you think that you would feel
  If they did it at the table?

If I had a stick,
   You'd think twice
Before you sat next to me
   And chewed your ice.

People frown and people stare
  At someone who plays with his silverware.

If there's something you want,
    And it's too far to grasp it,
Don't reach in front—
    Ask someone to pass it.

When done, don't push your plate away,
  Or stack your dirty dishes.
Your hostess will arrange to clear
  The dishes as she wishes.

Take knife and fork and place the two
  Across the plate to show you're through.

Even if you're through and itching to go,
Don't leave the table until you know
That you're excused to go play with Tom
By a signal from your host or Mom.

When you rise from the table,
Remember this bit:
Be careful, don't push
Or lean upon it.

And now, let's part with this, my friend,
　A little magic for the end.
Let's give the napkin one last cheer
　It makes everyone disappear.

When the hostess, with a smiling face,
　Replaces her napkin to its place
In napkin ring, or folded neat,
　And then arises from her seat
It's the signal that the fun
　Is over, and the meal is done.
And so you see, it is a fact,
　It is a disappearing act.